She Persisted

DIANA TAURASI

—INSPIRED BY—

She Persisted

by Chelsea Clinton & Alexandra Boiger

· ·

DIANA TAURASI

· ·

Written by

Monica Brown

Interior illustrations by

Gillian Flint

PHILOMEL

Philomel Books
An imprint of Penguin Random House LLC, New York

First published in the United States of America by Philomel Books,
an imprint of Penguin Random House LLC, 2022

Visit us online at penguinrandomhouse.com.

Library of Congress Cataloging-in-Publication Data is available.

Printed in the United States of America

HC ISBN 9780593402948
10 9 8 7 6 5 4 3 2 1
PB ISBN 9780593402962
10 9 8 7 6 5 4 3 2 1

WOR

Edited by Jill Santopolo and Talia Benamy.
Design by Ellice M. Lee.
Text set in LTC Kennerley.

To
Juliana Berglund-Brown
and female athletes everywhere

She
Persisted

....

She Persisted: MARIAN ANDERSON

She Persisted: VIRGINIA APGAR

She Persisted: NELLIE BLY

She Persisted: RUBY BRIDGES

She Persisted: CLAUDETTE COLVIN

She Persisted: ROSALIND FRANKLIN

She Persisted: TEMPLE GRANDIN

She Persisted: FLORENCE GRIFFITH JOYNER

She Persisted: HELEN KELLER

She Persisted: CORETTA SCOTT KING

She Persisted: CLARA LEMLICH

She Persisted: MAYA LIN

She Persisted: WANGARI MAATHAI

She Persisted: WILMA MANKILLER

She Persisted: PATSY MINK

She Persisted: SALLY RIDE

She Persisted: MARGARET CHASE SMITH

She Persisted: SONIA SOTOMAYOR

She Persisted: MARIA TALLCHIEF

She Persisted: DIANA TAURASI

She Persisted: HARRIET TUBMAN

She Persisted: OPRAH WINFREY

She Persisted: MALALA YOUSAFZAI

DEAR READER,

As Sally Ride and Marian Wright Edelman both powerfully said, "You can't be what you can't see." When Sally said that, she meant that it was hard to dream of being an astronaut, like she was, or a doctor or an athlete or anything at all if you didn't see someone like you who already had lived that dream. She especially was talking about seeing women in jobs that historically were held by men.

I wrote the first *She Persisted* and the books that came after it because I wanted young girls—and children of all genders—to see women who worked hard to live their dreams. And I wanted all of us to see examples of persistence in the face of different challenges to help inspire us in our own lives.

I'm so thrilled now to partner with a sisterhood of writers to bring longer, more in-depth versions of these stories of women's persistence and achievement to readers. I hope you enjoy these chapter books as much as I do and find them inspiring and empowering.

And remember: If anyone ever tells you no, if anyone ever says your voice isn't important or your dreams are too big, remember these women. They persisted and so should you.

Warmly,

Chelsea Clinton

DIANA
TAURASI

TABLE OF CONTENTS

....

Chapter 1: *Early Years* 1

Chapter 2: *Diana Becomes a Husky* 9

Chapter 3: *Going Pro* 18

Chapter 4: *Olympic Dreams* 24

Chapter 5: *Family* 33

Chapter 6: *Legacy* 41

How You Can Persist 48

References 51

Early Years

When Diana Lorena Taurasi was born on June 11, 1982, her parents didn't realize that she would one day be called a goat! The nickname "goat" had nothing to do with the animal, though. Diana would grow up to become a basketball GOAT—the **GREATEST OF ALL TIME**. Baby Diana grew to be tall like a tree, leaping and running and dribbling and shooting basketballs over other players' heads and into the basket.

All over the world, people would say that Diana Taurasi was one of the greatest basketball players of all time.

As a child, however, the sport Diana and her big sister, Jessika, learned about first was soccer. Diana grew up in Chino, California, but her parents, Mario and Liliana, were immigrants to the United States from Argentina, where soccer, called fútbol in Spanish, was *everybody's* favorite sport! Diana's family spoke only Spanish at home, and they ate delicious Argentinian food like BBQ with chimichurri sauce, yerba mate, and empanadas. Diana's father was born in Italy, but his parents had immigrated to Argentina when he was only five years old, so Diana was also influenced by her father's Italian heritage. Mario would leave at 4 a.m. to drive to his job operating machines in a big factory and not return home until 8 p.m., where his family was waiting for him to eat after his twelve-hour shifts. Meals were a special time for the Taurasi family, who loved to talk and eat and laugh together.

Diana's father was once a professional soccer player in Argentina, and there was *always* a soccer game on in the Taurasi home. Diana loved soccer and wanted to play all the time. But she loved basketball too, where she soared, leaping high and running fast on the court. Diana played basketball whenever and wherever she could—in driveways and parks, against boys and girls. She loved watching men's basketball on TV too, especially games featuring Magic Johnson, Michael Jordan, or Kobe Bryant! Diana's mother was a waitress and her father worked long hours, so it was difficult for her parents to take her to both soccer

and basketball practices. But they did it because she loved both sports so much, and they loved her.

Diana was an amazing basketball player—fast and smart on the court. Her graceful arms and hands could launch the ball straight into the basket and she could jump high! *Swoosh!* She reached 5'11" before she even became a teenager, and would one day grow to be six feet tall. Diana was confident and proud as she stretched toward the sky and her future as a basketball star!

Life in the United States wasn't always easy for the Taurasi family. It was hard to be so far from their family in South America and challenging to earn enough money to make ends meet. When Diana was twelve, her parents missed their family so much, they decided to move back to Argentina for a short time. In Argentina, Diana saw many people living in poverty. She saw children without shoes and people living in shacks made from iron sheets. The Taurasis lived in a dangerous neighborhood, where they were once robbed at gunpoint in their own home. The robber even took the basketball shoes off Diana's feet and put them on before he left! Thankfully, no one was hurt.

After her family moved back to California, Diana finally had to choose which sport she wanted to play most. Though she loved soccer, Diana and her family knew her greatest passion and most magical talent was for basketball, so she chose that path.

Diana, whose nickname was "Dee," was happiest on the court. She'd dreamed of playing basketball forever, but at that time there was no professional women's basketball association.

Female basketball players could compete in college, but then their careers would end. *Will things ever change?* Diana wondered. She looked to the men's NBA teams for inspiration and watched every Los Angeles Lakers game she could. During halftime and time-outs, she'd run outside to her driveway to practice the shots superstar Kobe Bryant made!

Diana joined Don Antonio Lugo High School's girls' basketball team, where she wowed everyone. And, of course, her family watched every basketball game they could, cheering her on! Games were fun and exciting when Diana was playing, because in addition to being fiercely competitive, she loved to have fun! Diana played with joy.

Coaches from all over California noticed Diana's talent. She was recruited to play for a team in the Amateur Athletic Union, then the all-stars! These were club teams made up of the most talented high school players across the country. Diana got to travel around the United States, competing and winning championships! As a high school player, Diana scored over three thousand points and led her team to many victories.

CHAPTER 2

Diana Becomes a Husky

The Women's National Basketball Association, the WNBA, was founded in 1996, the very year Diana Taruasi started playing basketball for Don Antonio Lugo High School. The NBA (the National Basketball Association) for men had been founded fifty years earlier in 1946. Now, as Diana had hoped, there was a way for talented women to play professionally! Her basketball career didn't have to end when she graduated college.

Diana could now dream of supporting herself and making a living doing what she loved. The women were paid far less than the men, which wasn't fair, but the new professional league was a step in the right direction. Diana had a new dream: become a WNBA player!

At Don Antonio Lugo High School, Diana led her team to many victories, often by making the winning shot at the very end of the game. Watching Diana was never boring. She could make layups and three-pointers and help other players shine with assists. She could rebound and steal balls from the opposing team, and she was wonderful at jump shots! She zipped off her shots low, keeping a space between herself and the basketball, tilting her feet a little to the left while jumping up and sending the ball flying through the air . . . *Swoosh!*

Diana's shots almost always went into the hoop!

Diana was a leader and liked to play point guard, which is a little like the quarterback position in football. She ran games, helping players get to the right place at the right time to score. She was also terrific in the shooting guard position—scoring

points and stealing the ball from other players! There seemed to be nothing Diana couldn't do with a basketball in her hand.

Diana Taurasi was the best high school basketball player in the entire country, and coaches from all over wanted her to play for their university. Where would she go? Her mother wanted her to stay close to home and go to UCLA. But when Diana was recruited by Coach Geno Auriemma of the University of Connecticut Huskies, she had to seriously consider the offer. Rebecca Lobo, one of Diana's basketball idols, had played for UConn, and during Diana's senior year of high school, the Huskies became the national women's college basketball champions for the 1999–2000 season, led by Sue Bird, who would one day become Diana's closest friend.

Coach Geno was an immigrant, born just thirty miles from Mario in Italy. He had a lot in common with Diana's parents. He promised to challenge Diana and help her learn even more about basketball. Diana decided to become a Husky!

When the time came, it was difficult to fly far away from her family to pursue her dreams. Diana had to adjust to the cold and snow of Connecticut and to Coach Geno's tough coaching style, but she didn't complain. Instead, she made jokes and worked even harder.

For the first few games of the 2000–2001 season, Diana didn't start, a new experience for her. In high school she was always asked to play first. Diana didn't like watching from the bench, but Coach Geno knew she had to earn her place as a starter. Playing with the very best players in the country, Diana learned quickly. When two experienced players were injured, she took a spot as a starter, vowing to become a team leader. Diana did just that, playing her best basketball ever, and leading the Huskies to the semifinals of the national college basketball championship tournament against Notre Dame.

It was a big game and Diana was under a lot of pressure. Then something happened to Diana that had never happened before. During the game, her confidence crashed. She couldn't score. Every ball missed the basket. She missed fourteen out of fifteen shots. When her team lost, Diana cried and cried. They were out of the finals. But did Diana give up after her biggest basketball disappointment? No! She persisted.

The next morning, Diana was back on the

court, practicing. She would do better and work on her physical and mental game. It didn't take long for Diana to get her confidence back. She was ready for her sophomore season!

The next year, Diana played alongside an all-star team that included Sue Bird, Swin Cash, Asjha Jones, and Tamika Williams—one of the most talented starting lineups of all time in women's college basketball. Diana Taurasi and Sue Bird became very good friends, though they didn't yet know how often their basketball destinies would cross in the future. The team shared a common goal: they wanted to become champions. They did it! Diana's hard work paid off! The Huskies won the National Collegiate Athletic Association (NCAA) Division I national championship the very next year! Diana had never been more excited or proud!

The next season, the senior stars had all graduated, and Diana, a junior, was the only remaining starter. Few believed that the Huskies could become champions again with only a junior as the team leader. But Coach Geno thought differently. Speaking of Diana, he said, "She elevates her teammates. She bestows greatness upon that. She convinces them that they're better than they've ever imagined to be." And once again, in 2003, the UConn Huskies became the NCAA women's basketball champions!

By Diana's senior year, everyone recognized the Huskies' most impactful player, with her long brown hair wrapped tightly in a bun at the top of her head and her big smile. Leading up to Diana's final championship, everyone wondered if the Huskies could have a three-peat, which is short for three repeated championships. Coach Geno simply said, "We've got Diana and you don't." Once again, Diana was under great pressure. But her confidence was high. She believed in herself and her teammates and led them to victory! The Huskies won and were once again crowned the NCAA women's basketball champions in 2004. The world had never seen a basketball player like Diana.

....

CHAPTER 3

Going Pro

Diana Taurasi, the best college basketball player in the nation, was about to graduate from the University of Connecticut. It was time for her to go pro with the WNBA! Diana Taurasi was named the number one draft pick by the WNBA. WNBA draft day aired on ESPN, and it was an exciting event! The top players from around the country were there, and Diana's parents and sister sat by her side as the new players were drafted.

The Phoenix Mercury had the number one pick, so of course they picked the number one player—Diana Taurasi! When Diana's name was called, she hugged her parents and everyone cheered. Diana would play for Phoenix and be much closer to her family. Phoenix summers were as hot as Connecticut winters were cold, which is to say—very hot! But no matter where she played, Diana's head was always cool, and her game was on fire!

On draft day, Diana joked to the camera that male basketball players like LeBron James and Carmelo Anthony didn't have to wear heels and "be uncomfortable" on draft day. Later on, Diana realized that she didn't need to wear heels either, ever again. She even wound up wearing tennis shoes to her own wedding!

Diana made a huge impact on the Phoenix

Mercury. Her very first year as a professional player, she led the team in scoring. She was very competitive and loved to win, win, win. And Diana had learned how to work hard from her parents. When the Mercury lost, Diana didn't get mad at her teammates—instead she encouraged them and led by example. On every team she played on, her teammates got better. Diana loved every aspect of the game of basketball—from working out at the gym, to joking with her teammates in the locker room, to battling it out on the court during a game. Diana seemed to thrive under pressure and led the Phoenix Mercury to their first WNBA championship in 2007!

She went on to break record after record, raising the profile of women's basketball and changing the game forever. Diana often played against Sue

Bird, her UConn Huskies teammate, who played for another WNBA team, the Seattle Storm, where she too was leading her team to WNBA championships. Even though Diana was becoming more famous, appearing on the cover of *Sports Illustrated* and other magazines, she never forgot where she came from. She treated every fan with respect and always made time to sign autographs and talk to young basketball players who wanted to grow up to be just like Dee!

With Diana Taurasi in the lead, the Phoenix Mercury won two more WNBA championships in 2009 and 2014, supported by players like Penny Taylor, Cappie Pondexter, Candice Dupree, and Brittney Griner. During the 2014 finals, Diana, Brittney, and Candice were nicknamed the "Big Three" players, crucial to beating the Chicago Sky for the WNBA championship. It seemed like Diana could make any shot from anywhere on the court. *Swoosh!* She could pass behind her back and score while being fouled. Watching Diana was fun for everyone because she played with style, flair, and the skill of an acrobat.

Diana never gave up her love for soccer either, and this was reflected in her amazing footwork as a basketball player. Often, after basketball practice, Diana would play fútbol with anyone who was left

on the court! Diana even named her dog Messi after the great Argentinian soccer player Lionel Messi. Diana would love soccer all her life, but basketball *was* her life.

CHAPTER 4

Olympic Dreams

Diana was recruited to play for the US Olympic Women's Basketball Team. She officially became an Olympian at only twenty-two years old when she played for Team USA at the 2004 Olympics in Athens. As the child of two cultures and three continents—Europe, South America, and North America—seeing so many nations come together for sports was an amazing experience for Diana. Once again, she was surrounded by the very best players in the world. Diana did her part as Team USA played Team Australia for the gold medal, and Team USA won! Diana Taurasi, along with her friend Sue Bird, went on to win three more gold medals in the 2008 Beijing Olympics, the 2012 London Olympics, and the 2016 Olympics in Rio de Janeiro. The Olympics were both fun and magical, and there Diana got to know many of the male basketball players she idolized, including Kobe Bryant, who saw that Diana's confidence came from practicing how she played! Diana took her daily practices as seriously as games played in front of television cameras.

Diana achieved so much, but she refused to stop dreaming. In 2020, she wanted to play in her fifth Olympics. Could Diana Taurasi win a fifth gold medal in her late thirties, when most players

had already retired? Could she make the team? Diana, who knew how rough basketball could be on her body, had changed her lifestyle to extend her sports career, becoming a vegan and training in new and creative ways. Because of the COVID-19 pandemic, the 2020 Olympics were delayed by one year. Of course Diana decided to go for it, saying, "It's not about you. It's not how good you are. It's how good can you be playing with other great players." She was joined once again by her best friend, Sue Bird. Could they help Team USA earn another Olympic gold in Tokyo and break another record? Time would tell.

Winning was important, but it was just as important to Diana and Sue to protect and promote female Olympic athletes. The US Olympic Women's Basketball Team is one of the most dominant teams ever, and along with the US Olympic Men's Basketball Team, they make up an Olympic basketball dynasty! Yet during the year, female basketball players have to struggle in ways male players do not—especially with low salaries.

Despite how talented many woman athletes are, they are paid less than male athletes, an unfair reality across every professional sport. Because pay is so low for female basketball players in the United States, many athletes feel they have to go abroad to Europe to play during the WNBA off-season to earn money to support themselves and their families. For most of her career, Diana played for teams in Russia and Turkey, adding six EuroLeague championships to her list of basketball honors. It was hard to be so far from her family, and Diana only had a week of vacation each year. She didn't have time to recover before flying abroad to play basketball and secure her economic future. Diana and Sue played together in Russia and became even closer.

One evening, during the long lead-up to the Olympic Games in 2021, Sue, Diana, and their agent, Lindsay, were having dinner together, talking about the struggles that woman basketball players face in the United States, especially as they age, because they aren't allowed time to rest and train in the off-season like professional male athletes. Sometimes, they would get injured and have to sit out the WNBA season in the United States. Or even the Olympics!

Diana and Sue brainstormed and got more and more excited. Women are powerful, they thought, and it was time for female athletes to be recognized and appreciated. They needed a pen and paper to write things down! They couldn't find a pen, but Lindsay, who had a toddler, managed to find a purple crayon in her purse, and Sue and Diana started planning.

They asked themselves, *How could the WNBA and US Olympics better support female athletes?* Diana and Sue wanted USA Basketball to help create a better future for its players. They decided to ask the WNBA and the US Olympic program to protect the health of their athletes so they could play longer. History was written that night in crayon!

Sue and Diana used their fame to help all players. They persisted in highlighting unequal treatment in women's sports until they were victorious! Two of the best basketball players of all time,

Olympians with four gold medals apiece at the time, negotiated successfully with USA Basketball to offer better contracts for every member of the US Olympic Women's Basketball Team. These Olympians would be paid more so that they could choose to stay in the United States to train in the WNBA off-season if they wanted. And by doing so, they could inspire the next generation of athletes.

It was a good beginning. And to top it all off, Diana and Sue joined the US Olympic Women's Basketball Team at the Tokyo Olympics, where they won gold! Diana and Sue became the only basketball players ever, of any gender, to win five Olympic gold medals! Afterward, the press couldn't tell if Diana was joking when she said, "See you in Paris!" where the next Summer Olympics would be held.

CHAPTER 5

Family

The same year the Phoenix Mercury recruited Diana, they also recruited a talented Australian player, Penny Taylor, who had been playing for both the WNBA team the Cleveland Rockers and the Australian national team. Diana Taurasi and Penny Taylor met on the first day of training camp for the Phoenix Mercury in 2004. They were Phoenix Mercury teammates for ten seasons and were fellow Olympians, where they played against each other—Diana for the USA, and Penny for Australia. They were the only two Mercury players who were part of all three of the team's WNBA championships. Penny was a smart and gifted player, and she and Diana soon became close friends and eventually girlfriends. Penny and Diana had a great partnership on and off the court.

On May 13, 2017, Diana and Penny were married in front of family and friends. Diana described her and Penny's wedding day as "one of the happiest we've ever had!" Unfortunately, there are still people who discriminate against samesex couples. A journalist asked Penny about what public reaction might be to their wedding, and she replied, "I would hope people would be happy for two people that love each other. At the end

of the day, it's pretty simple." Penny retired from professional basketball in 2017 and was honored by her former coaches, her former teammates, the Phoenix Mercury community, and of course, Diana, who noted not only her talent on the court but also the way she treats others, always with dignity and respect.

In 2018, Diana and Penny had a son, who they named Leo Michael Taurasi-Taylor. Becoming a mother filled Diana with a new type of love. Until little Leo was born, her life had mostly revolved around basketball. But when her son first opened his eyes and looked at her, Diana's life was changed. Now after basketball practice, Diana would rush home to play with Leo and take him to the park and on scooter rides as he grew. When baby sister Isla was born a few years later, she was presented with

a gift from Diana and Penny's basketball family: a baby onesie that said FUTURE GOAT!

With Penny and Diana as parents, will Leo and Isla want to play basketball? Or soccer? Will they be dancers or doctors or teachers? Will they stretch up tall as trees and arc the ball high across the court? What kind of GOATs will they become? Certainly they will grow up as Diana and Penny did, loved by parents who want them to be happy and pursue their dreams. As Diana has said, she followed her passion and her love of the game, and from that joy and a lot of hard work, beautiful things grew, because "when you do it with love and passion, a lot of great things can happen for you."

In addition to being a great player herself, Diana has inspired many young women to play basketball and pursue their dreams. One young athlete who Diana inspired was Gigi Bryant, the daughter of basketball star Kobe Bryant. After Kobe retired from the Lakers, he began coaching his daughter and would often ask for tips from Diana. They became great friends. In one inter-view Bryant talked about the day when WNBA players would join the all-male NBA, and Diana Taurasi was at the top of his list of women players who could. Kobe knew that girls like his daughter Gigi had benefited from the struggles, accomplishments, and breakthroughs of Diana and other female athletes. Gigi Bryant's dream was to follow in her idol Diana Taurasi's footsteps and become a University of Connecticut Husky! Gigi got to know Diana, who recognized Gigi's fierce determination and the sense of belonging and excitement the young player found on the court.

When Kobe, Gigi, and other young basketball players and their family members died in a helicopter crash on the way to a game in early 2020, Diana was devastated. At their memorial service, Diana shared how she learned one of her signature moves from Kobe, and that she still ends each workout with that move: "Three hard dribbles going right. Left foot plant, pivot, swing right leg through. Elevate, square up, follow through." Diana also honored Gigi Bryant. With tears in her eyes, Diana noted that Gigi had represented the future of women's basketball, when "a young girl doesn't require permission to play. Her skill would command respect."

With the loss of her young friend, Diana was even more motivated to create better opportunities for female basketball players, and she worked for gender equity, which means equal opportunities for and treatment of people regardless of their gender, in the WNBA and on the US Olympic Women's Basketball Team.

Legacy

Adecade before Diana was born, in 1972, Congress passed a law called Title IX, which made it illegal to treat women unfairly in educational settings funded by the federal government. This helped ensure college sports like women's basketball were funded, allowing young Diana the incredible experience of playing on an outstanding and well-supported college team.

Title IX protected women and girls in public

high schools and colleges, but Diana wanted to create change in the world of professional and Olympic sports. So she persisted. Diana Taurasi used her fame and her platform to fight for investment in women's sports, especially the game she loved—basketball. Diana's persistence in talking about inequities in her sport at every opportunity helped change attitudes that affect woman athletes and non-athletes alike. Even so, there is more work to do to close the gap in wages between men and women in the world of sports and beyond.

Diana Taurasi was never selfish on the basketball court. If she saw another player had a better shot, she passed the ball—often without even looking, to trick her opponent! Diana wasn't selfish off the court either. She fought for better pay and equal treatment not only for herself but for

all female basketball players in the United States. Diana brought attention to the unequal treatment of women in sports, and fought for recognition and respect for all female athletes. She also inspired love for the game through the beauty and style with which she played it.

Diana spent her life as an athlete becoming the best basketball player she could be. She worked constantly to improve, practiced hard, supported her teammates, and led every one of her teams to great victories. Her basketball skills were dazzling, and this, along with her fiercely competitive spirit, led her to three WNBA championships with the Phoenix Mercury, five Olympic gold medals with Team USA, six EuroLeague championships, and six ESPY Awards for excellence in sports performance. She became the all-time leading scorer in the WNBA, one more reason she has been called the greatest of all time.

Diana Taurasi is still persisting and still dreaming, and continues to build on what is already an amazing legacy. In 2021, less than two months after winning the gold in Tokyo, Diana found herself once again in the WNBA semifinals. At thirty-nine years old, still healing from injuries and limping at times, Diana beat her own all-time scoring record in a playoff game, making eight three-pointers for a total of thirty-seven points! She also became the oldest player in WNBA history with a thirty-point game.

When asked who the best women's basketball player of all time was, Diana Taurasi, always modest, refused to claim the title, noting that there have been many good players. Her friend Sue Bird, who had played by her side as a Husky, in Russia, and at five Olympics, disagreed and pointed to Diana, saying, "That's what you say when you are the best player." Sue went on to say that what makes Diana Taurasi the true GOAT is not only the championships and the winning but the joy in her game. "There's something about her style that's infectious. Whoever's on the court with her raises their game. I think, for me, that's why she's the GOAT."

The WNBA celebrated its twenty-fifth season in 2021. They sponsored a "Vote for the GOAT!" contest. WNBA fans voted Diana Taurasi, the WNBA all-time leading scorer and

Phoenix Mercury guard, the league's greatest player of all time!

Diana Taurasi, the young girl who loved both fútbol and basketball, who spoke both Spanish and English, grew up strong and tall as a tree. With a basketball in her hand, she ran, jumped, and sent the ball flying toward the net. On team after team, she shot, scored, passed, and made plays. Pressure and competition brought out the best in her. She loved the game of basketball and tried to make her sport more fair for the girls and women who would come after her.

Diana Taurasi, born in the United States to Argentinian and Italian immigrants, raised in a working-class town in California, grew up to become the GOAT! *Swoosh!*

HOW YOU CAN PERSIST

by Monica Brown

If you admire Diana Taurasi and would like to help carry on her legacy, there are a few things you can do.

1. Attend a women's basketball game! Help boost attendance at your local high school, college, or professional women's sports competitions.

2. Get moving and get to a basketball

court! Head to your local park or the hoop over a friend's garage. Practice dribbling and shooting, alone or with friends! With a friend, you can practice passing. With a group, you can play a game!

3. Visit the Women's Basketball Hall of Fame in Knoxville, Tennessee! You can also visit the museum from home: wbhof.com/about /museum-from-home. Learn more about those who have contributed to the sport of women's basketball at all levels!

4. Try out different sports. Diana played both soccer and basketball when she was young. Why not give a new sport a shot? You could try running, soccer, softball, gymnastics, or basketball! What other sports interest you?

5. You've learned a lot about Diana Taurasi. Go to your local library and do some research about other female athletes. Find out more about Simone Biles, Bethany Hamilton, Dara Torres, Serena Williams, or Megan Rapinoe, to name a few.

6. Diana believed in teamwork, and she liked and respected her teammates very much. They supported each other. Make sure you have a team of people who support you and who you support.

7. Share Diana Taurasi's story with your friends and family. Tell them about her amazing basketball skills, and tell them that she has fought to bring equality and visibility to women's basketball.

∽ References ∾

ARTICLES

Bushnell, Henry. "Changed the Game: Meet the
Radical Agent-Activist behind Sports' Most
Inspiring Stories." Yahoo! March 3, 2021.
yahoo.com/lifestyle/womens-history-wnba
-agent-lindsay-kagawa-colas-changemaker
-180510760.html.

Conley, Kevin. "Be Like Dee." *The New Yorker*.
February 29, 2004. newyorker.com/magazine
/2004/03/08/be-like-dee.

Deford, Frank. "Geno Auriemma + Diana Taurasi = Love, Italian Style." *Sports Illustrated*. November 24, 2003. vault.si.com /vault/2003/11/24/geno-auriemma-diana -taurasi-love-italian-style-a-pair-of-paisans-at -uconn-share-a-passion-for-hoops-that-makes -a-perfect-match-of-cocky-coach-and-fearless -player.

Metcalfe, Jeff. "Mercury Star Diana Taurasi Marries Former Mercury Player Penny Taylor." *The Arizona Republic*. May 15, 2017. azcentral.com/story/sports/wnba/mercury /2017/05/15/phoenix-mercury-star-diana -taurasi-marries-former-mercury-player-penny -taylor/321798001/.

Metcalfe, Jeff. "Sue Bird and Diana Taurasi
Talk Olympics, NCAA Tournament Inequities
and Controversial No-Call in UConn's Win."
The Arizona Republic. March 30, 2021.
usatoday.com/story/sports/ncaaw/2021/03/30
/sue-bird-diana-taurasi-olympics-wnba-ncaa
-tournament-uconn-baylor/4814768001.

Mizell, Gina. "Diana Taurasi Is Still Living
Up to Her 'White Mamba' Nickname." *The
New York Times.* September 15, 2020. nytimes
.com/2020/09/15/sports/basketball/diana
-taurasi-is-still-living-up-to-her-white-mamba
-nickname.html.

Pelton, Kevin. "Sue Bird Endorses Diana
Taurasi as WNBA's GOAT amid League's

25th Anniversary Celebration." ESPN.
September 7, 2021. espn.com/wnba/story
/_/id/32168239/sue-bird-endorses-diana-taurasi
-wnba-goat-amid-league-25th-anniversary
-celebration.

Rohlin, Melissa. "Kobe Bryant and Diana Taurasi
Shared a Deep Mutual Respect." *Sports
Illustrated*. May 27, 2020. si.com/nba/lakers
/news/kobe-bryant-and-diana-taurasi-shared
-a-deep-mutual-respect.

Valdez, Gino. "Big Three Dominant as Mercury
Set Fire to Sky." *Northeast Valley News*.
September 7, 2014. nevalleynews.org/853
/sports/big-three-dominant-as-mercury-set
-fire-to-sky.

VIDEOS

"All Access: Diana Taurasi and Alana Beard on
Draft Night." WNBA, May 13, 2016. Video,
2:59. youtube.com/watch?v=v6tWLvLBt2Y.

"Diana Taurasi Shooting Form: WNBA Shooting
Secrets." Shot Mechanics, July 7, 2017. Video,
3:38. youtube.com/watch?v=QMI4-9CyI8o.

"WNBA Players Sue Bird and Diana Taurasi on
New Contract." CBS Mornings, January 29,
2020. Video, 6:27. youtube.com/watch?v=rEv
-hMa-I6Y.

WEBSITES

"2001–02 Connecticut Huskies Women's Basketball
Team." Wikipedia. Accessed January 25, 2022.

en.wikipedia.org/wiki/2001%E2%80%9302
_Connecticut_Huskies_women%27s_basketball
_team.

"About Diana Taurasi." DianaTaurasi.com.
Accessed February 10, 2022. dianataurasi
.com/about.

"National Basketball Association." Encyclopedia
Britannica. Accessed February 10, 2022.
britannica.com/topic/National-Basketball
-Association.

"Title IX." Women's Sports Foundation. Accessed
February 10, 2022. womenssportsfoundation.org
/advocacy_category/title-ix.

DR. MONICA BROWN is the award-winning author of many multicultural books for children, including *Frida Kahlo and Her Animalitos*; *Sharuko: El Arqueólogo Peruano/Peruvian Archaeologist Julio C. Tello*; *Waiting for the Biblioburro/Esperando el Biblioburro*; *Marisol McDonald Doesn't Match/ Marisol McDonald no combina*; *Small Room, Big Dreams: The Journey of Julián and Joaquin Castro*; and the Lola Levine chapter book series. Her books have garnered multiple starred reviews and awards, and have been featured by *The New York Times*, *The Washington Post*, and NPR's *All Things Considered*. She is a professor of English at Northern Arizona University and lives in Flagstaff with her family.

Photo credit: *Cameron Schmitz*

You can visit Monica online at
monicabrown.net
and follow her on Twitter
@monicabrownbks

GILLIAN FLINT has worked as a professional illustrator since earning an animation and illustration degree in 2003. Her work has since been published in the UK, USA and Australia. In her spare time, Gillian enjoys reading, spending time with her family and puttering about in the garden on sunny days. She lives in the northwest of England.

You can visit Gillian Flint online at
gillianflint.com
or follow her on Twitter
@GillianFlint
and on Instagram
@gillianflint_illustration

CHELSEA CLINTON is the author of the #1 *New York Times* bestseller *She Persisted: 13 American Women Who Changed the World*; *She Persisted Around the World: 13 Women Who Changed History*; *She Persisted in Sports: American Olympians Who Changed the Game*; *Don't Let Them Disappear: 12 Endangered Species Across the Globe*; *It's Your World: Get Informed, Get Inspired & Get Going!*; *Start Now!: You Can Make a Difference*; with Hillary Clinton, *Grandma's Gardens* and *The Book of Gutsy Women*; and, with Devi Sridhar, *Governing Global Health: Who Runs the World and Why?* She is also the vice chair of the Clinton Foundation, where she works on many initiatives, including those that help empower the next generation of leaders. She lives in New York City with her husband, Marc, their children and their dog, Soren.

Courtesy of the author

You can follow Chelsea Clinton on Twitter
@ChelseaClinton
or on Facebook at
facebook.com/chelseaclinton

ALEXANDRA BOIGER has illustrated nearly twenty picture books, including the She Persisted books by Chelsea Clinton; the popular Tallulah series by Marilyn Singer; and the Max and Marla books, which she also wrote. Originally from Munich, Germany, she now lives outside of San Francisco, California, with her husband, Andrea, daughter, Vanessa, and two cats, Luiso and Winter.

You can visit Alexandra Boiger online at
alexandraboiger.com
or follow her on Instagram
@alexandra_boiger

Read about more inspiring women in the

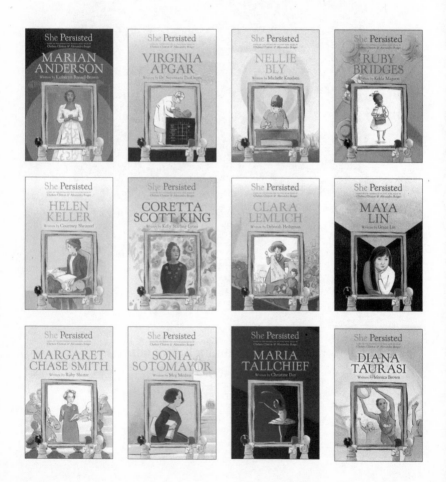